RMS TITANIC

COLOURING BOOK

First published 2016
Reprinted 2019, 2020

The History Press
97 St George's Place,
Cheltenham, Gloucestershire, GL50 3QB
www.thehistorypress.co.uk

Text © Steve Hall & Bruce Beveridge, 2016
Illustrations by Lucy Hester © The History Press, 2016

British Library Cataloguing in Publication Data.
A catalogue record for this book is available from the British Library.

ISBN 978 0 7509 7850 7

Cover colouring by Lucy Hester
Typesetting and origination by The History Press
Printed and bound in Turkey by Imak.

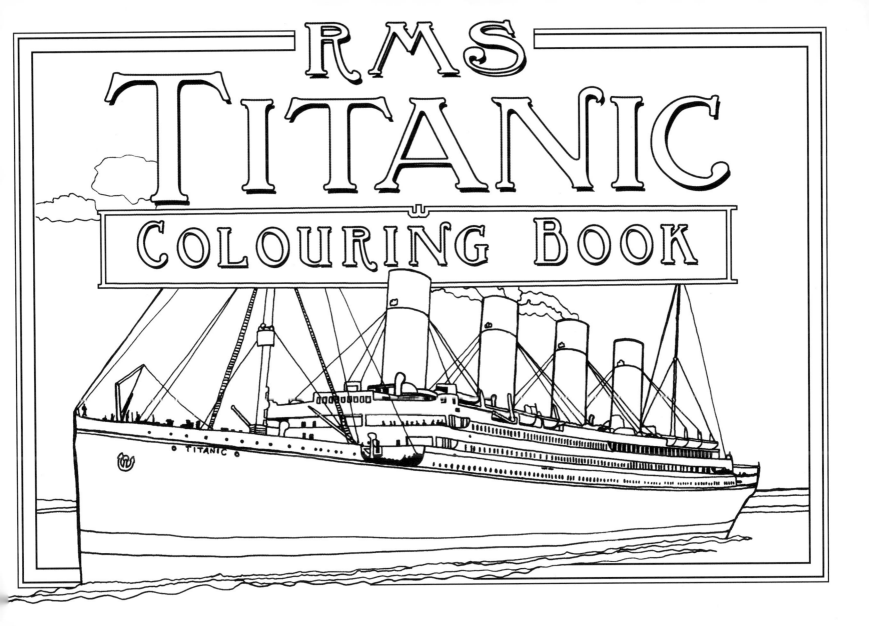

Before the jet aircraft, the only way to travel across the ocean was on board a ship, on a journey taking several days. Most Atlantic passengers were emigrating from Europe to America, generally poor, and travelling in simply furnished third-class accommodations. Between 1901 and 1910 over 8 million immigrants landed at New York, and in competing for passengers, steamship companies commissioned ever larger and faster ships.

Titanic and her sister ship *Olympic* were built at the Belfast shipyard of Harland and Wolff for White Star Line, completely eclipsing the Cunard Line's *Mauretania* and *Lusitania* both in luxury and size. *Olympic* and *Titanic* had all of the upscale amenities of the finest hotels on land, as well as a gymnasium, Turkish baths, a squash court and a heated saltwater swimming pool. White Star's policy was to emphasise accommodations over speed.

Titanic's keel was laid on 22 March 1909. She was constructed from the same plans as *Olympic* and mirrored her construction schedule, though seven months behind. The cost for both ships was £3 million for the pair, Harland and Wolff's usual arrangement with White Star being 'cost plus 3 per cent'. The

White Star Line put out advertising to the public and shipbuilding community in anticipation of *Olympic* and *Titanic*, well aware potential passengers would be attracted by the cachet attached to sailing on either of these two vessels, then the largest ships in the world. *Titanic* was 46,328.57 gross registered tons (grt), a measurement of internal volume. If you could have placed *Titanic* on scales, she would have weighed 51,240 tons when departing Southampton.

passenger capacity for the Olympic-class liners was generally 735 first-class, 674 second-class and 1,026 third-, or steerage-, class passengers. Including crew, *Titanic* was certified safe for the transportation of 3,547 people.

On 31 May 1911 *Titanic* was launched, in just sixty-two seconds. Drag chains, steel hawsers and anchors were used to arrest the backward movement of her massive hull and to bring it to a standstill once afloat. Following her launch, *Titanic* was taken in tow by five tugs, which escorted her to the deep-water outfitting wharf. Here all her heavy propulsion machinery, funnels and other equipment, along with her interiors, would be fitted. The sisters had four huge funnels rising 72ft above the Boat Deck, painted black at the top to mask the smoke residue. The fourth funnel was only for ventilation. It is often asked, why four funnels if only three were needed? Three reasons: it was more aesthetically pleasing; it gave the illusion of power and stability; and it followed the four-funnel arrangement of White Star Line's competitors.

On 3 February 1912 *Titanic* was dry-docked. Over the following two weeks the three giant propellers were fitted and the hull below the waterline cleaned and painted. After successfully completing her sea trials on 2 April, *Titanic* departed for Southampton, arriving late the following evening and docking alongside Berth 44 just after midnight.

On Wednesday 10 April, at 12.15 p.m., *Titanic* slowly eased away from her berth. She steamed 77 nautical miles across the English Channel, arriving at the French port of Cherbourg the same evening. Just after 8 p.m. she departed for Queenstown (known today as Cobh) on the south coast of Ireland, anchoring in Cork Harbour just before noon the following day. Just after 1.30 p.m. *Titanic* weighed anchor for the last time, before steaming out into the Atlantic, tracking westward for New York.

We all know what happened next. The first lifeboat came alongside *Carpathia* at 4.10 a.m. and the last at 8.15 a.m. With all 712 survivors on board (1,496 missing), the rescue vessel steamed to New York, arriving on the evening of 18 April. The wreck of *Titanic* was finally discovered on 1 September 1985.

The purpose of this book is not to dwell on the disaster, but rather to showcase the beautiful ship that *Titanic* all too briefly was, and to breathe life once again into the timeless vessel and the era she represented.

Steve Hall and Bruce Beveridge

With the advent of the newest and largest steamers in the world, White Star Line had much to be proud of. Promotional booklets were printed to illustrate the luxurious appointments with some in magnificent colour. The brochure this advertisement came from illustrated interiors and scenes from the ships' construction – their boilers and watertight doors that caused the maritime community to label these ships 'practically unsinkable'.

WHITE STAR LINE

Royal & United States Mail Steamers.

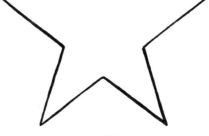

"OLYMPIC" & "TITANIC"

45,000 TONS EACH

The Largest Vessels in the World.

May 1911

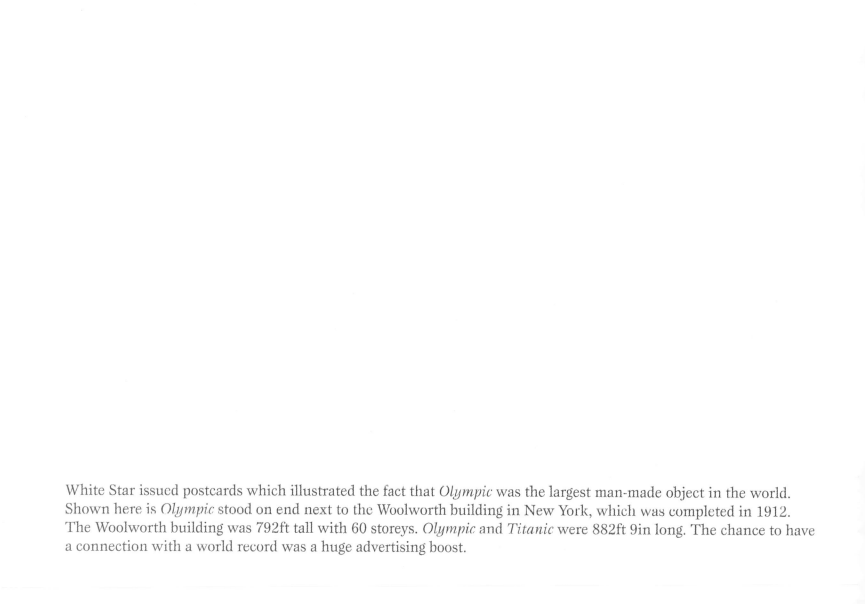

White Star issued postcards which illustrated the fact that *Olympic* was the largest man-made object in the world. Shown here is *Olympic* stood on end next to the Woolworth building in New York, which was completed in 1912. The Woolworth building was 792ft tall with 60 storeys. *Olympic* and *Titanic* were 882ft 9in long. The chance to have a connection with a world record was a huge advertising boost.

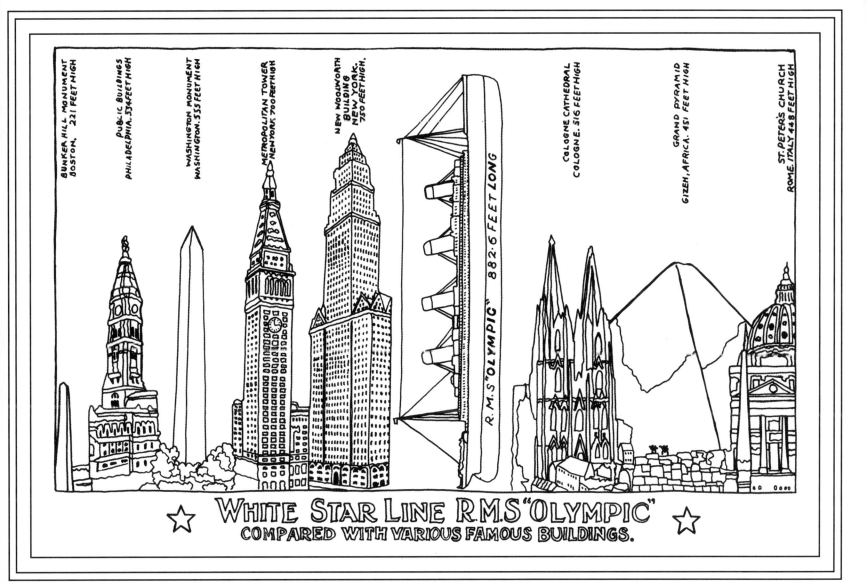

BUNKER HILL MONUMENT
BOSTON, 221 FEET HIGH

PUBLIC BUILDINGS
PHILADELPHIA, 535 FEET HIGH

WASHINGTON MONUMENT
WASHINGTON, 555 FEET HIGH

METROPOLITAN TOWER
NEW YORK, 700 FEET HIGH

NEW WOOLWORTH BUILDING
NEW YORK, 750 FEET HIGH.

R.M.S "OLYMPIC" 882·6 FEET LONG

COLOGNE CATHEDRAL
COLOGNE, 516 FEET HIGH

GRAND PYRAMID
GIZEH, AFRICA, 451 FEET HIGH

ST. PETER'S CHURCH
ROME, ITALY 448 FEET HIGH

★ WHITE STAR LINE R.M.S "OLYMPIC" ★
COMPARED WITH VARIOUS FAMOUS BUILDINGS.

Able to boast of the newest and largest steamers in the world, White Star Line took every opportunity to promote the exclusivity of these ships. As seen in this period illustration, the focus is clearly directed towards third-class passengers. This card was for *Olympic*, which entered commercial service on 14 June 1911 and remained one of the most popular passenger steamships through her twenty-year career. *Olympic* was scrapped in 1935 during the Great Depression.

Titanic's centre anchor was the largest in the world at the time and manufactured by the firm of Noah Hingley & Sons Ltd, of Netherton, Dudley. It weighed just over 15¾ tons and was housed on the Forecastle Deck abaft the stem.

Titanic's wing propellers each had three manganese-bronze blades fastened on to a cast-steel boss, and had a diameter of 23ft 6in. The wing propellers were driven by *Titanic*'s massive reciprocating engines while the centre propeller was powered by a steam turbine. The centre propeller was four bladed and of solid construction, cast of manganese bronze with a diameter of 17ft. Unlike the wing propellers, it could not be operated in reverse.

The steam which powered *Titanic* was generated by twenty-four double-ended and five single-ended coal-fed boilers. Each double-ended boiler was 15ft 9in in diameter and 20ft long, while the single-ended boilers were of the same diameter but 11ft 9in long.

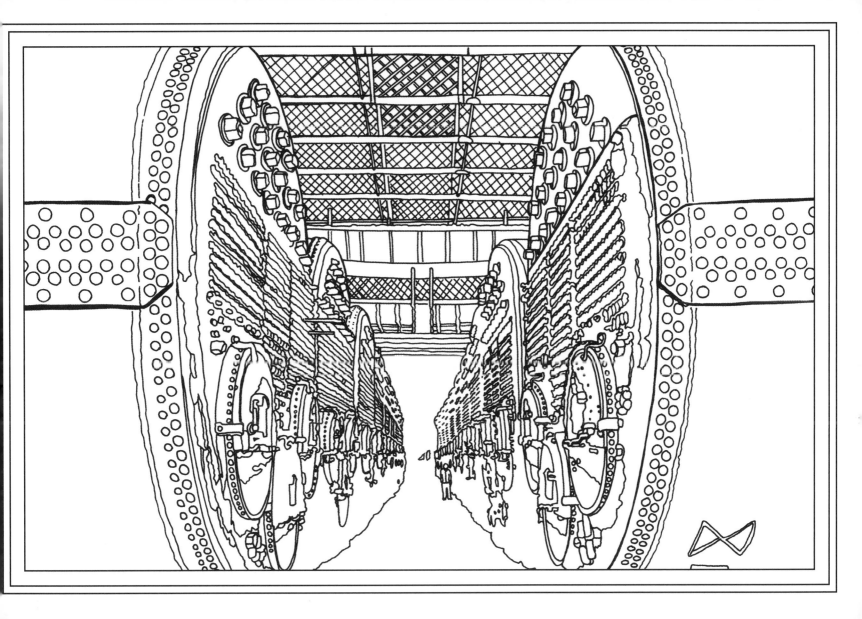

Titanic stands proudly awaiting her launch. The observation stands were constructed for those privileged enough to receive a special invitation. Soon over 100,000 people gathered around the shipbuilding yard at Harland and Wolff, and along the banks of the Victoria Channel, to watch her take to the water for the first time.

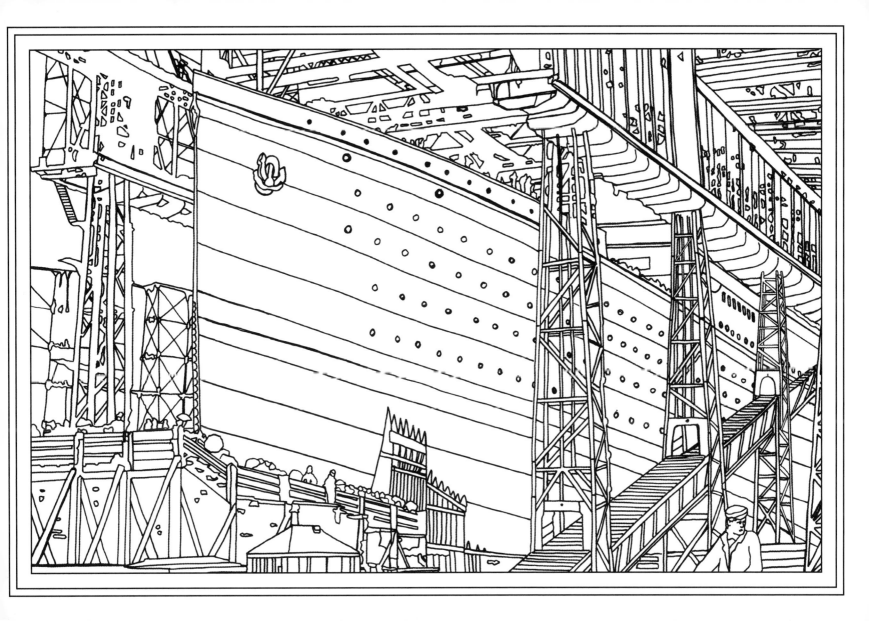

Titanic's hull slid stern first into the water on 31 May 1911. It took just sixty-two seconds for the ship to slide down the ways and into the water. *Titanic* reached a speed of 12 knots and came to a complete stop within her own length.

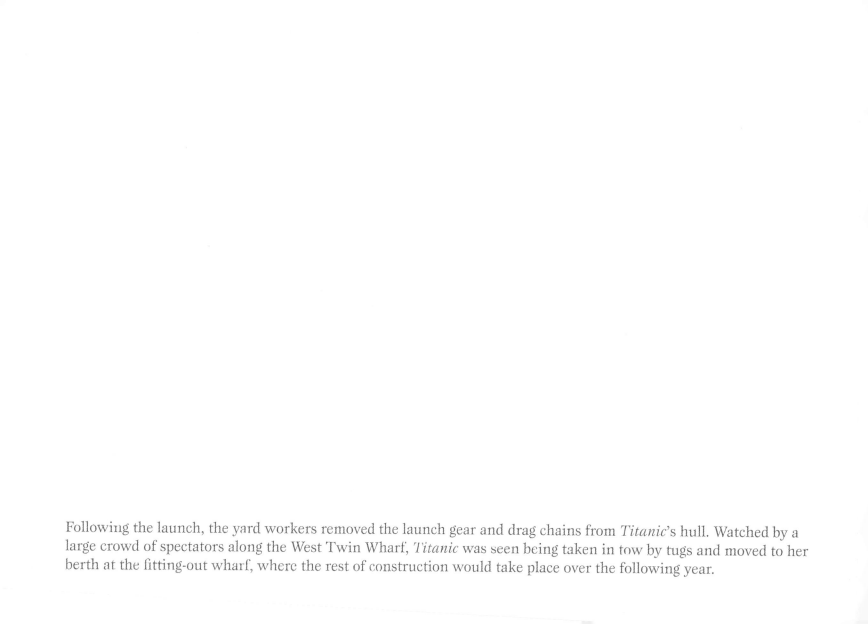

Following the launch, the yard workers removed the launch gear and drag chains from *Titanic*'s hull. Watched by a large crowd of spectators along the West Twin Wharf, *Titanic* was seen being taken in tow by tugs and moved to her berth at the fitting-out wharf, where the rest of construction would take place over the following year.

Titanic was put in the dry dock in March 1912 to have her three propellers put on their shafts and the paint applied to her hull below the waterline. The dry dock was owned and operated by the Belfast Harbour Commission and was the only one large enough for ships of the Olympic class. Its concrete walls were 18½ft thick and had a line of 332 massive keel blocks along its centre-line to support the ships within when the water was drained out.

With *Titanic* in dry dock and her sister *Olympic* tied up alongside in the fitting-out wharf immediately behind, she was a spectacular sight looking down from one of the shipyard cranes in March 1912. *Titanic* was now just three weeks away from her sea trials.

Before *Titanic* was officially handed over to her owners, she underwent sea trials. *Titanic* was guided out of Victoria Channel by tug boats around 9.30 a.m. on 2 April. From the channel, *Titanic* sailed on her own until her engines and machinery were found to be in working order. The trials had been set down to commence the previous day, but were postponed due to inclement weather.

Titanic finished her sea trials and returned to Belfast at 6.30 p.m. That same evening, the British Board of Trade's representative, Francis Carruthers, signed the certificate of seaworthiness, valid for one year, and certified her for the transportation of 3,547 passengers and crew. The transfer of the vessel from builder to owner was then official.

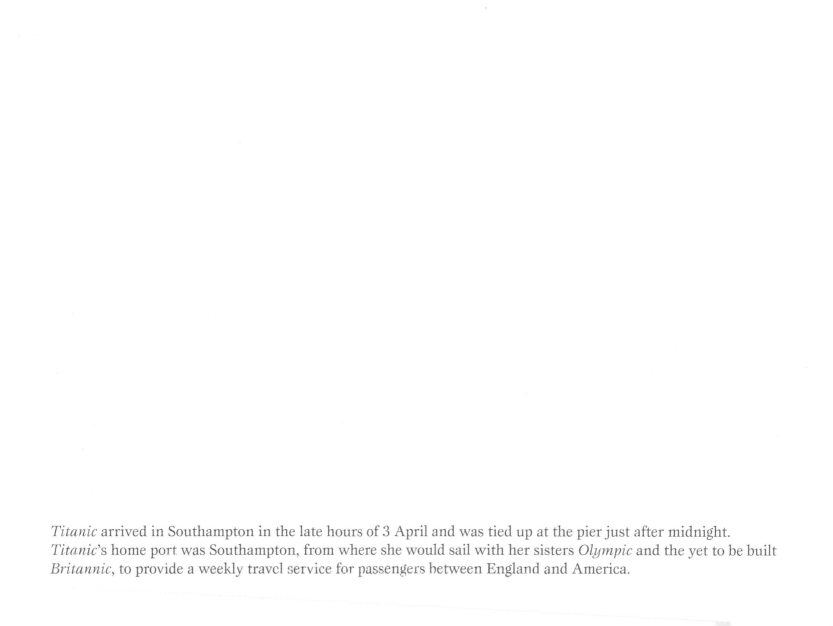

Titanic arrived in Southampton in the late hours of 3 April and was tied up at the pier just after midnight. *Titanic*'s home port was Southampton, from where she would sail with her sisters *Olympic* and the yet to be built *Britannic*, to provide a weekly travel service for passengers between England and America.

White Star Line assigned its most senior and respected caption for *Titanic*'s maiden voyage, Captain Edward John Smith. Captain Smith had commanded many of White Star Line's new ships in the past. His last command was *Olympic*, but he had also served on earlier flagship vessels such as *Majestic* and *Adriatic*. Smith was popular with his passengers. He was very personable and, with his white beard and stocky figure, he looked like the stereotypical ship's captain. Smith was sixty-two years old and it was rumoured that he was to retire following *Titanic*'s maiden voyage.

Captain Smith and his six navigating officers, Chief Officer Henry Wilde, First Officer William Murdoch, Second Officer Charles Lightoller, Third Officer Herbert Pitman, Fourth Officer Joseph Boxhall, Fifth Officer Harold Lowe and Sixth Officer James Moody, commanded *Titanic* from the navigating bridge. It is from here that the officer of the watch would use telegraphs to signal speed commands down to the engineers far below decks, and control the ship's whistles. The ship's wheel in the Navigating Bridge was used when *Titanic* was leaving or coming into port with the compass binnacle located right in front of it. There is no known photograph of this area on *Titanic* but her bridge was nearly identical to that of her sister *Olympic*. In this view, the telegraphs, binnacle and wheel are visible, as well as other ancillary equipment.

On Wednesday 10 April 1912, *Titanic* was ready to take on passengers. The first to come aboard were first class followed by second class and finally third. One of the first awe-inspiring sights to greet the first-class passengers was the magnificent grand staircase with its beautiful panelling in English oak, and the attractive wrought-iron and glass skylight dome above. The staircase was the largest of two in first class, being forward in the ship, and traversed seven decks. At the very top landing was mounted a wooden sculpture of two figures around a clock called 'Honor and Glory Crowning Time'. All of the first-class recreation areas and staterooms could be reached by this staircase or, if one chose to avoid stairs, there were three elevators available.

The first-class gymnasium was open for ladies and gentlemen free of charge between 10 a.m. and 6 p.m., and children between 1 p.m. and 3 p.m. It was provided with both traditional exercise equipment and what were considered, in 1912, to be the latest electric exercise appliances.

The swimming bath was a luxury, and was not yet a common feature aboard ships at the time. It was 33ft long, 14ft wide and with a depth of between 4ft 6in and 5ft 4in. Due to the dirty water in port, the heated saltwater pool would not be filled until *Titanic* reached the clean open waters of the Atlantic.

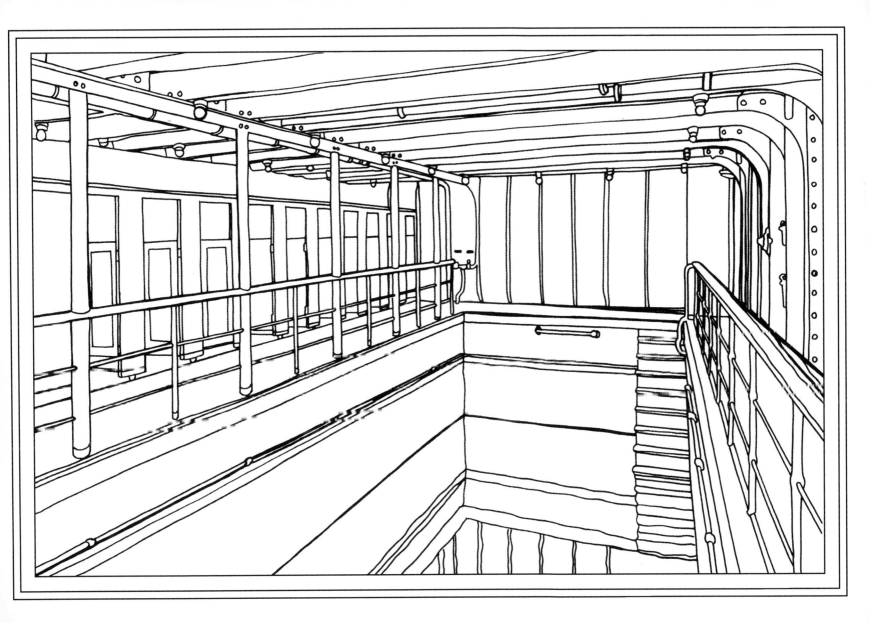

The Turkish baths were available for ladies from 10 a.m. to 1 p.m., and for gentlemen from 2 p.m. to 6 p.m. Tickets could be purchased from the enquiry office for $1 each. Bathers liked to weigh themselves before and after a Turkish bath to see how much weight they had lost. The walls were tiled in large panels of pale blue and green, and the floor was covered with blue and white 'lino' tiles laid over Litosilo.

First-class stateroom B64 was only one of four staterooms aboard *Titanic* with a canopy bed. It was decorated Empire style with white and gilt panelling inset with crimson silk damask panels and a moulded white and gilt ornamental ceiling. This stateroom is not known to have been occupied during the voyage.

First-class stateroom B60 was decorated in the stunning Queen Anne style of carved and highly polished mahogany panelling with silk damask panels of an old gold colour. Incorporated into the panelling was an imposing 8ft-wide mahogany fitment of two wardrobes flanking a double lavatory unit.

First-class stateroom B59 was decorated in Old Dutch style, with a panelled, carved and inlaid dark oak dado with an embossed and decorated lincrusta frieze above. The ceiling was executed in embossed white panels separated by carved oak beams. Like B64, it is not known to have been occupied during the voyage.

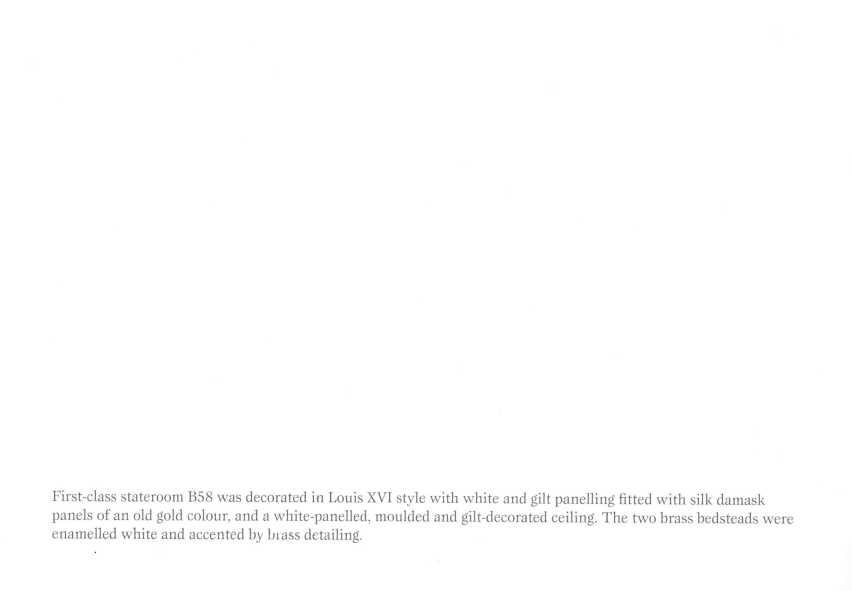

First-class stateroom B58 was decorated in Louis XVI style with white and gilt panelling fitted with silk damask panels of an old gold colour, and a white-panelled, moulded and gilt-decorated ceiling. The two brass bedsteads were enamelled white and accented by brass detailing.

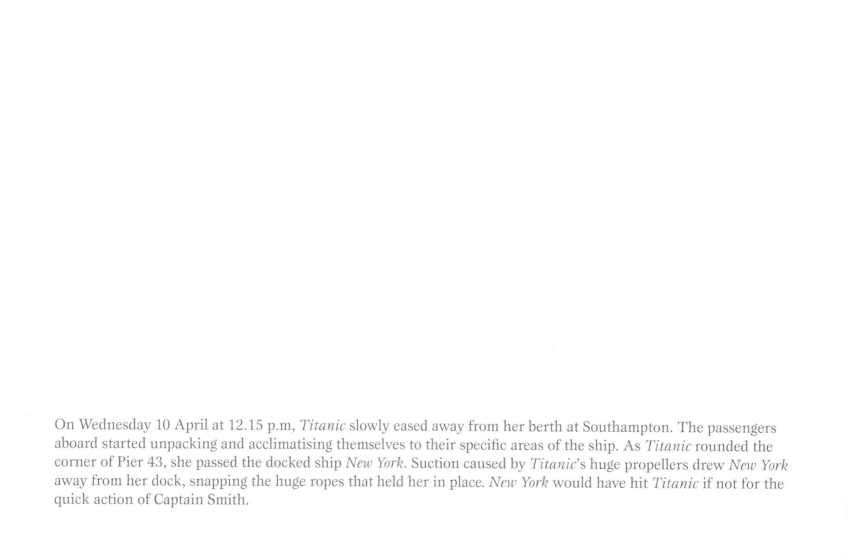

On Wednesday 10 April at 12.15 p.m, *Titanic* slowly eased away from her berth at Southampton. The passengers aboard started unpacking and acclimatising themselves to their specific areas of the ship. As *Titanic* rounded the corner of Pier 43, she passed the docked ship *New York*. Suction caused by *Titanic*'s huge propellers drew *New York* away from her dock, snapping the huge ropes that held her in place. *New York* would have hit *Titanic* if not for the quick action of Captain Smith.

Titanic was guided by tugs while leaving the White Star dock in Southampton. When she was clear of other ships moored nearby and it was safe for her to sail under the power of her own engines, the tugs let her off the ropes. The Olympic-class liners were so large that the waterways and channels around Southampton and New York had to be dredged so that they were deep enough to handle them.

As *Titanic* proceeded down Southampton Water, she passed a number of smaller craft, offering a perfect comparison to *Titanic*'s enormous size. The decks were temporarily deserted as lunch was being served. At *Titanic*'s bow an anchor was lowered to the waterline in case it was needed to slow the forward motion of the ship if there was a need to stop.

The first-class passengers had their first meal on *Titanic* on 10 April while sailing from Southampton to Cherbourg. Their dining saloon was an immense facility, by far the largest afloat at the time. It was decorated in early seventeenth-century Jacobean, the style of which was drawn from Hatfield, Haddon Hall and other great English houses that were noted examples of the Jacobean period. The floor was laid with multicoloured 'lino' tiles, and the chairs upholstered with pale green leather.

The first-class Café Parisien was an entirely new luxury innovation aboard *Titanic*, and offered diners a view of the ocean. The overall appearance of this room was intended to be that of a French sidewalk café. The long, narrow room had wicker furniture, large rectangular windows and walls accented with trained ivy and other plants climbing the trellis-work panelling. The Café Parisien was attached to the à la carte restaurant, where passengers had the choice of food offerings from a menu, and had to pay the bill just like a restaurant on land.

The second-class dining saloon accommodated 394 passengers and extended across the full width of the ship. It was an elegantly decorated room of a style that only a few years previously had been considered suitable for first class. Amidships at its forward end, the saloon surrounded the forward second-class staircase and foyer on three sides, with a door on either side opening into the foyer from the dining area. The carved oak chairs were upholstered with red padded seats.

Third-class accommodations aboard *Titanic* were basic, but they were worlds apart from the conditions emigrants had endured in years gone by. Just twenty years earlier, the third class would never have dreamed of enjoying white tablecloths or of being served by waiters. The food was regulated by the British Government, and White Star's 'Bill of Fare' exceeded even the minimal dietary requirements. Just as in first and second class, there was a smoking room with a bar for third-class male passengers, while the women and families could relax in the adjoining general room.

When the third-class passengers were not promenading on deck or taking their meals, they had the option of staying in the third-class general room, located at the aft end of the ship. This room was panelled and framed in pine, and finished in white enamel, with the floor covered with red and white 'lino' tiles. Hung on walls around the room were posters advertising ships and routes of the various steamship lines owned by White Star Line's parent company, the International Mercantile Marine. On the other side of the ship was the similarly decorated third-class smoking room. Third class enjoyed the same types of public rooms as first and second class, only less ornate.

As *Titanic* sailed the 77 nautical miles between Southampton and Cherbourg, passengers had an opportunity to promenade the open and spacious decks provided for their specific class. First-class passengers were allowed on the topmost deck, or Boat Deck, for promenading. The deck just below, called A Deck, consisted of a long and spacious promenade along the length of the public rooms inside, where first-class passengers could rent deckchairs if they decided to lounge away the time.

Both Royal Mail and US Mail were exchanged from *Titanic* at Cherbourg and Queenstown. Passengers could receive their mail, after it was sorted, at the purser's office, located in the main companionway of their respective class. The second-class purser's office was plainly panelled in contrast to first class, but it was as elegant as a concierge desk in some of the finest hotels on land. Located on E Deck, opposite the landing of the after second-class staircase, this purser's office was panelled in oak and fitted with three windows where passengers could make enquiries. Also provided was a post box and a brochure rack.

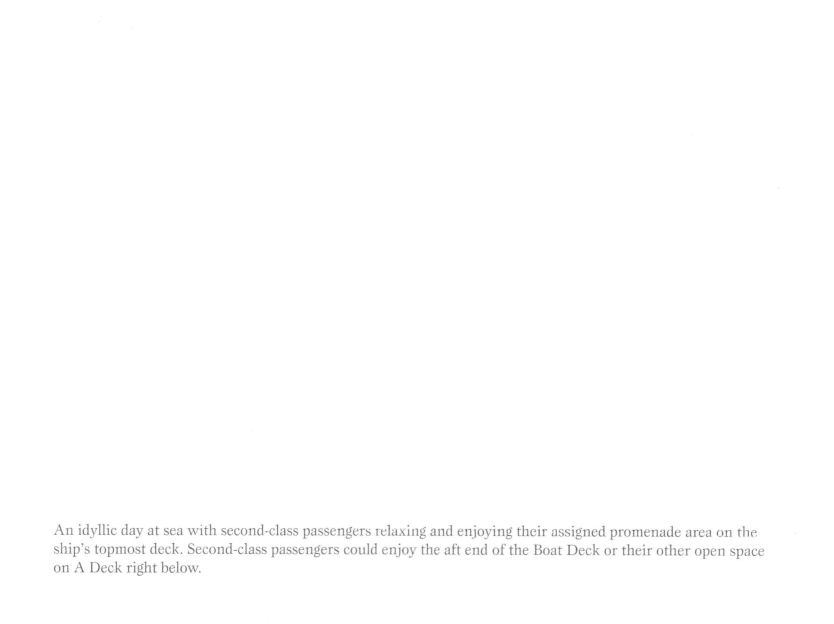

An idyllic day at sea with second-class passengers relaxing and enjoying their assigned promenade area on the ship's topmost deck. Second-class passengers could enjoy the aft end of the Boat Deck or their other open space on A Deck right below.

It took almost a whole week to cross the Atlantic on ships like *Titanic*. To pass the time, passengers wrote letters, played cards, walked, lounged and, when weather permitted, they played deck games on the open decks. Shuffleboard was played on the raised roof over the first-class smoking room. Players used a long wooden stick to shove India-rubber discs on to squares marked with the highest numbers, while at the same time endeavouring to knock an opponent's discs off the numbers.

Deck quoits were popular, and there were several ways of playing. In one variation, passengers were to attempt to throw rope rings (quoits) on to pegs; another was to toss them into numbered squares chalked on to the deck; a third method was to try to see which side could get the most quoits nearest to a single chalk mark.

After the evening repast, first- and second-class passengers would usually attend music concerts put on by the ship's orchestra in the main companionways of their respective class. The men would look forward to fine cigars and conversation in the smoking rooms, which were not intended for women. *Titanic*'s first-class smoking room was arguably the most lavish compartment on the ship, decorated with dark carved wood and stained glass, with semi-private alcoves and a genuine coal-burning fireplace. Above the fireplace was a painting by Norman Wilkinson called *Approach to the New World*. The flooring was of a red-and-blue pattern. The colour of the leather on the furniture is uncertain; it may have been green, or perhaps burgundy to match the tiles.

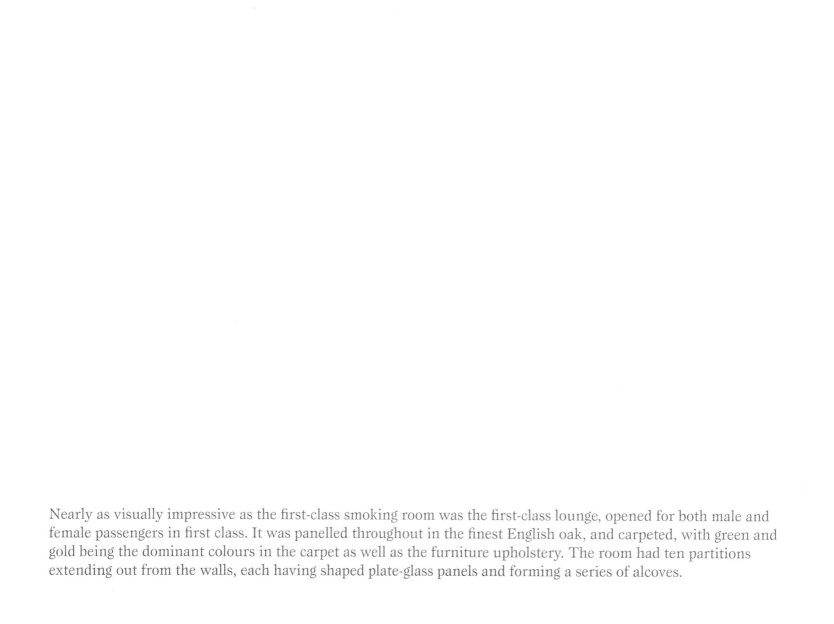

Nearly as visually impressive as the first-class smoking room was the first-class lounge, opened for both male and female passengers in first class. It was panelled throughout in the finest English oak, and carpeted, with green and gold being the dominant colours in the carpet as well as the furniture upholstery. The room had ten partitions extending out from the walls, each having shaped plate-glass panels and forming a series of alcoves.

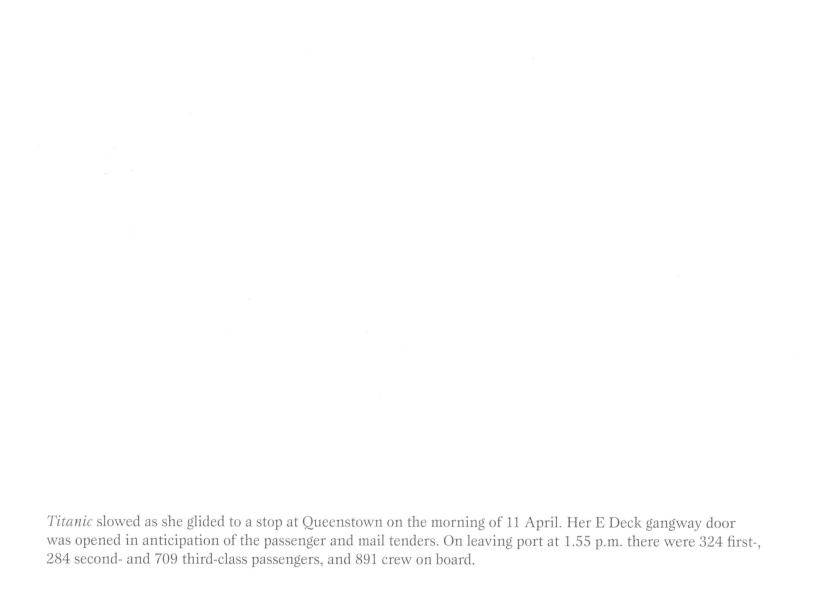

Titanic slowed as she glided to a stop at Queenstown on the morning of 11 April. Her E Deck gangway door was opened in anticipation of the passenger and mail tenders. On leaving port at 1.55 p.m. there were 324 first-, 284 second- and 709 third-class passengers, and 891 crew on board.

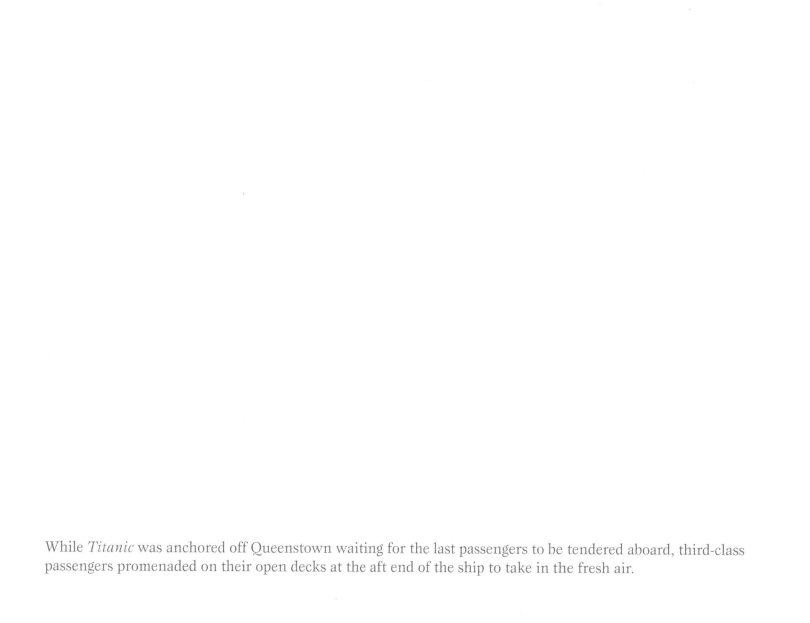

While *Titanic* was anchored off Queenstown waiting for the last passengers to be tendered aboard, third-class passengers promenaded on their open decks at the aft end of the ship to take in the fresh air.

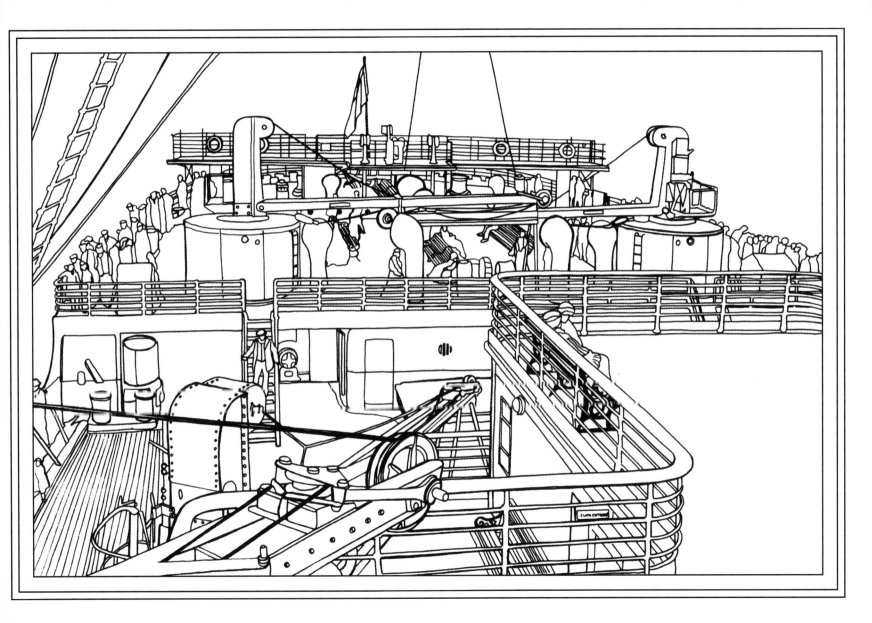

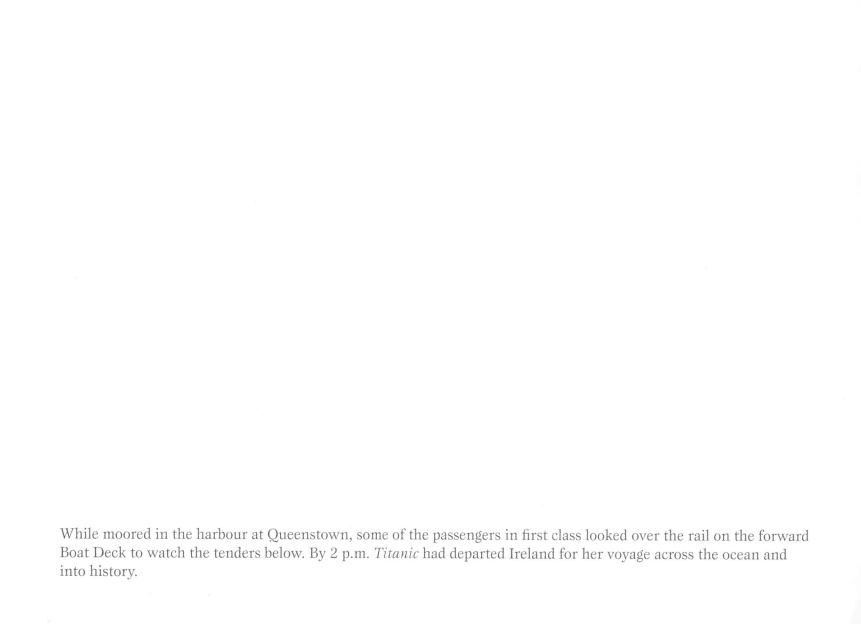

While moored in the harbour at Queenstown, some of the passengers in first class looked over the rail on the forward Boat Deck to watch the tenders below. By 2 p.m. *Titanic* had departed Ireland for her voyage across the ocean and into history.

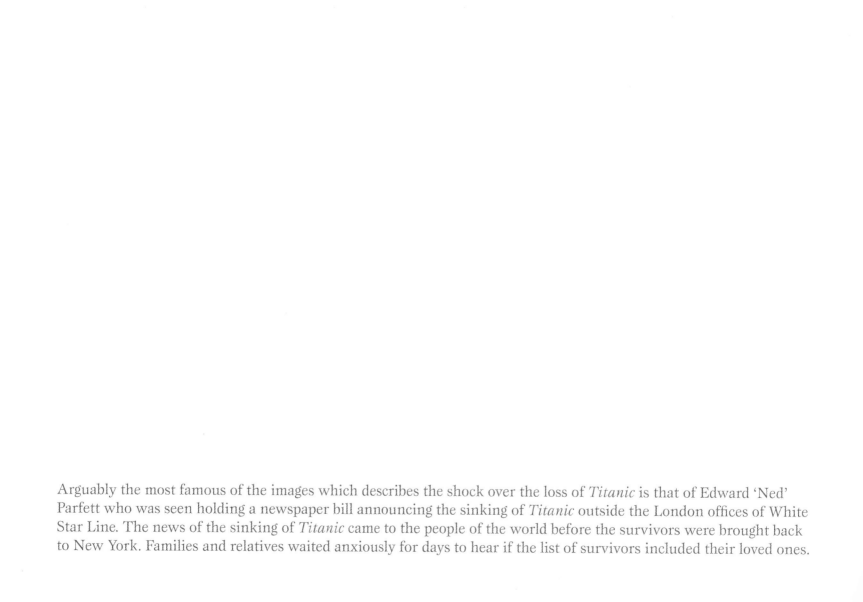

Arguably the most famous of the images which describes the shock over the loss of *Titanic* is that of Edward 'Ned' Parfett who was seen holding a newspaper bill announcing the sinking of *Titanic* outside the London offices of White Star Line. The news of the sinking of *Titanic* came to the people of the world before the survivors were brought back to New York. Families and relatives waited anxiously for days to hear if the list of survivors included their loved ones.

The twin-screw Cunard steamship *Carpathia* was the ship that raced to *Titanic*'s rescue. In command at the time was Captain Arthur Henry Rostron. The first of *Titanic*'s lifeboats came alongside *Carpathia* at 4.10 a.m. and the last at 8.15 a.m on 15 April. With all 712 survivors on board, *Carpathia* steamed to New York, arriving on the evening of 18 April 1912.

The wreck of *Titanic* was finally discovered on 1 September 1985, *c.* 370 miles (595km) south-south-east off the coast of Newfoundland at a depth of 12,460ft (3,797m) approximately.

Also from The History Press

978 0 7524 9774 7

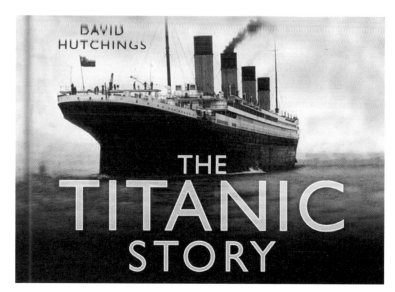

978 0 7509 4845 6